CHAPTER 1

Understanding what, where, how and why you have chosen to disappear.

"Even if you're not doing anything wrong, you are being watched and recorded." - Edward Snowden

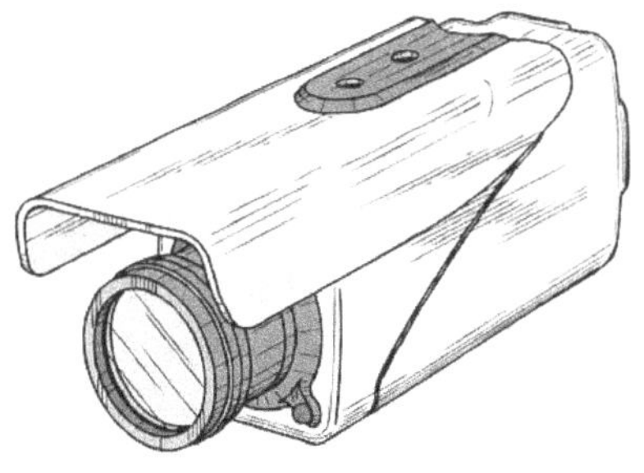

Walking away from your present life and identity is by far the most profound and significant change you as an individual can make, it directly affects all your family, professional, nonprofessional, and peripheral relationships.

There are many times when choosing to disappear and not be found are a matter of personal survival, not some lust for adventure. If you are in an abusive relationship and you fear for your life and possibly the life of your child, you may not have very many options other than escape from your situation.

It is not suggested, you take a child or children with you while you are on the run, instead take the child to a neighboring state and seek help. It is important that you have documentation to back up your abuse accusation. Police reports, medical reports, photographs etc. This information will assist you in getting a new social security number; this is covered in detail in chapter 3.

It is not fair, but women and children have more shelter resources available to them than men with kids in similar circumstances. If you take a minor child that is not in an abusive or dangerous situation without court approval, you will become a high priority capture to local, state, and federal law enforcement agencies.

You might be well meaning but taking a kid without legal sanction is dangerous to you and emotionally damaging to the child. Sometimes we contact a class of people who have no problem making you disappear in the wrong way, loan sharks, drug dealers and other very bad people.

You do not have to owe these people anything, if they perceive that you know more about their business than they want you to, you could have a serious problem. If you are thinking, I will have the police protect me. "Good luck" law enforcement agencies exist to catch bad people after they commit a crime. Do you really want to wait around to become a victim so you will be a higher priority to your police agency?

We humans are not perfect; we make many mistakes, some insignificant, some major. If your mistake was criminal in nature, this book will be of limited value to you. It does not offer any advice on how to be an effective fugitive, law enforcement agencies have unlimited resources and will never stop searching for you.

Probably somebody or some corporate entity will look for you, the length of time and intensity of the search based on their motivation to find you and assets allocated for that purpose. The importance of understanding the resources and motivation of the person or agency looking for you cannot be overstated.

If your problem is an abusive spouse, girlfriend, boyfriend, or you just want to reboot your life and drop off the grid for a while, you can accomplish that with thoughtful and careful execution of the plans laid out in this book.

People make mistakes, poor choices, and bad decisions, that said; in a perfect world every adult should honor every contract they enter be it verbal or written. However, if the contract is morally indefensible, an example would be usury rates on money loaned or a contract to provide or engage in illicit or criminal activity, you will have to decide if you can do what you promised to do under duress.

Almost everyone has heard of or read the urban legend about the man who tells his wife he is going to the corner store for a pack of cigarettes and never returns or he returns 20 years later, depending on what version of the story you are familiar with. The reason this story is mentioned is it tends to illustrate the deep-seated yearning that most people have for adventure and to seek answers to life's what ifs?

Your life belongs to you; pay limited attention to people who make judgments about you following societal norms or anything like that. If you are unhappy with the way things are going, you can shuffle the deck of life and deal yourself a new hand.

Despite what most people would say, to disappear and not be found, is not crazy; it very well could be one of the most rational choices you could make.

 You certainly have heard the adage "Doing the same thing over and over but expecting the results to change is insanity."

This is mentioned because sometimes life tends to drop you into deep valleys for "lack of a better way to describe it" bad luck, rotten karma etc.

Now it is time for the rubber to hit the road, get yourself a legal pad or paper of some kind and divide it in half by drawing a line down the center of the paper.

On one side of the paper write all the reasons and benefits of disappearing from your present life. The opposite side of the paper is used to list the reasons to continue your life as is.

Regardless of your choice, you should read this book because it will teach you techniques to protect your privacy and other civil liberties that most people take for granted.

You will also learn to recognize the technologies that corporations and government use to collect personal data about you and effective strategies to avoid giving it.

CHAPTER 2

How to Disappear from the Internet.

"There are no secrets on the Internet."

— *Paul Babicki*

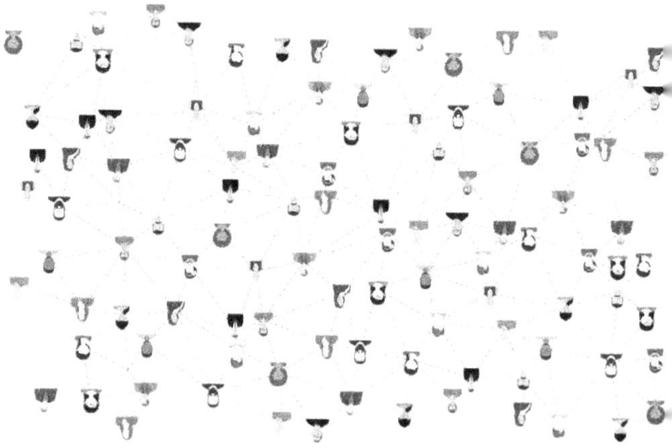

Disappearing from the physical world in some ways is easier than vanishing from the internet; luckily, the internet contains lots of repetition in the content.

Your personal information is harvested and sold repeatedly to marketers and data-mining companies, propagating like a virus, in fact the term "going viral," means data of some kind being rapidly disseminated around the internet.

The reason to erase yourself from the internet is its use as the default reservoir holding a pool of information about you, it also is the primary tool used by professional and amateur sleuths.

As you start the process of identity removal, you are going to be shocked at the amount and scope of your personal information available to anyone with an internet connection.

This part of your plan will require patience and perseverance on your part and a certain level of cooperation from the internet companies that are archiving your personal information. There are only about a dozen major websites that comprise the backbone of the personal data collection business, the thrust of your effort should be to remove your personal information from the major players because most of the smaller websites operating in this realm mirror the information collected by the top personal information aggregators.

Compile a list of every website you can remember joining, registering, participating in etc., this list should include email accounts, school, college, or any other academic institution.

 If you are an athletic booster; you are on a list, colleges and universities will have a specific protocol for delisting from their databases.

You should try their website first, then possibly a phone call or letter may be required.

Today's video game industry is more profitable and larger than the motion picture industry, a large percentage of video games require registration of some kind. You will have to remove all your information from the game website, and you will have to get rid of all virtual items you have acquired by selling or giving them to other players. If you have a blog or personal website, you need to close it down, if you own a domain name, you can let it expire, sell, or give it away.

You also need to close accounts that host third party accounts and or web applications designed to work with websites like Facebook, Instagram etc.

 Check with your cell phone provider to determine if your phone number is a part of an online directory, if it is, have the company remove it.

Delete your personal information from online advertisement websites like Craigslist and any other similar websites, the similar websites will most likely be local or regional publications. Search engines are the way people find things on the internet and that is where someone or some agency looking for you will go to first, removing yourself from search engines will usually require offline contact via fax or certified return receipt letter, this is required to establish your identity.

There are enough search engines that have information about you; it will save time and effort by constructing a template used to draft letters requesting delisting from their search engine database.

This is a list of the more relevant search engines; this list is not all-inclusive, but you will go a long way in removing your information from the internet by concentrating on these search engines:

.www.yahoo.com,

www.bing.com

www.whitepages.com

www.USsearch.com

www.Intelius.com

www.ZabaSearch.com

www.acxiom.com

www.PeopleFinder.com

www.google.com

Close or cancel all free email accounts like Hotmail, Gmail, and Yahoo Mail etc. If you use some type of cloud storage, cancel the account after you safely retrieve your data and archive it again, under a different name.

There are places that will be extremely difficult or impossible to have your personal information expunged, newspapers, radio, and other media outlets that you have willingly given interviews or have been the subject of a story or article will be reluctant to comply with your request.

Another place you will have problems purging information from is government; federal, state, or local. The information that is collected is customarily considered part of the public domain; this includes property tax records, voter registration, drivers' license, utility company records etc.

The mother lode of personal information is contained in the databases of the major social media websites; these websites contain names, dates, photos and information about your hobbies, friends, family members, employment, even your religious preference.

The social networking websites need to be a high priority in your plan to vanish, you must cancel your membership in all of them because if you leave one open eventually your information will be everywhere again.

This list of the major players in the social media world is not all-inclusive; however, it will take you a long way in removing your personal data from the internet.

www.FaceBook.com

www.Twitter.com

www.YouTube.com

www.Flickr.com

www.Linkedin.com

www.StumbleUpon.com

www.eBay.com

You need to remove yourself from all newsletters and mailing lists; it is not enough to cancel your email account because your information will live on in the databases of the entities sending you the newsletters and mailers.

If you must correspond with personnel that work for the website that you want your data to be removed from; remember the adage "you catch more flies with honey than with vinegar" all this means is remember you are talking to a human being and nobody likes to be yelled at or threatened.

In the beginning of this chapter and throughout this book the point has been made repeatedly; this process of vanishing done correctly takes time and perseverance, however it is possible to contract this phase of the plan out.

There are professional companies that will remove your information from the internet for a fee; the advantages in using a company that specializes in this type of service are many.

You free yourself from the burden of committing the large amount of time this process requires; a professional company may have proprietary methods and contacts with data providers and legal muscle at their disposal.

CHAPTER 3

Plan To leave and leave nothing behind.

"It's none of the government's business where innocent citizens are, what they're doing or what they're thinking."

— *Danny Mekić*

After you make the decision to leave your life behind, you need to decide where in the world you want to go.

It should be a place where people who know you would believe "that is the last place on earth he/she would go to." This phase of your plan will take about 3 to 4 months to implement.

It is not recommended that you go to a large city because large urban areas are more heavily monitored with CCTV security and law enforcement surveillance, you also should stay clear of small towns and villages where you would "stand out" as an outsider and draw undue suspicion.

The ideal location is a medium sized city. A new name will be needed for your new identity, pick a very common name; John or Jane Smith or something along that line, if you Google those names, you will find many entries.

That is exactly what you want; you want to hide in plain sight. A legal name change does not cost much money; you can get the forms and do it yourself.

After you get your name changed, update your driver's license to reflect your new name, then buy a prepaid Visa or MasterCard with your name printed on the card, add a library card to the mix and you have enough basic identification to get you going.

If you look on the internet you will find articles that tell you to adopt the identity of an infant or child that was born about the time you were born but died very early in life.

This might have been a good strategy years ago; however, it is a very risky thing to do today.

There is no way to know if a felon or con artist has beaten you to that identity and law enforcement or collection agencies are searching for that person.

It is very likely that death information is monitored by federal law enforcement agencies.

The world changed after 9/11, computational power is cheap, and memory is even cheaper, it does not make sense to invite the hassle and unpredictable outcome of using a dead person's identity.

You will need to get rid of stuff connected to you but do it in a way that does not arouse attention; that means canceling all subscriptions to magazines, newspapers, and other periodicals. If you have data on a personal computer, it is not gone just because you deleted it.

The only way to be certain that no information about you is gleaned from your computer's hard disk is to remove it, immerse it in boiling water for at least 10 minutes, beat it with a hammer and finally drill holes in the hard disk.

I know this might appear to be a little over the top, but the computer forensic field is very sophisticated and good technicians are able to accomplish some amazing things in the data recovery arena.

If you have small debts, pay them; If they are too large to pay consider chapter 7 bankruptcy to discharge the debts, before your name change.

You do not want a debt collector to inadvertently find you and ruin your plans, "the fewer people looking for you the better off you are".

If you have assets now is the time to start converting them to cash, sell your stocks, bonds, mutual funds, and any other financial instrument.

If you jointly own property with another person, forget about cashing it in or appropriating it for your exclusive use.

It does not belong to you exclusively and minimally it will create problems in the short term, "nobody wants to feel like they have been stolen from" and it may be illegal in your state.

You must get rid of as much personal memorabilia as you can, your books, music, photos, trophies etc. tell a potential sleuth a great deal about your habits, likes, dislikes and numerous other things that could make it easier to find you.

In the event you are escaping a potentially violent partner you need to place as many obstacles in their path as possible, if you can, disable the vehicle they would use to pursue you. The best way to do this is to put grits or oatmeal in the radiator of the vehicle, you can also put sand into the engine where oil is put.

A potato shoved into the exhaust pipe will also keep a car engine from running, the potato must fit tightly; use a stick or something to push it into the exhaust pipe out of obvious view.

If you have access to the household money, you are entitled to your half. You will need it to help finance a fresh start, take the other half, and place it with an attorney instructing the attorney to place it in escrow for 60 days or so and then disburse the funds.

You have not taken what you are not entitled to, all you have done is placed a speed bump in the path of your primary pursuer.

If the person you are getting away from has a stash of firearms you should remove the bullets or magazine also called a clip and deposit the guns in any

US Postal System mailbox or place them in a container and notify the police telling them the location of the container.

Make the call from a pay phone or a disposable cell phone, it does not matter what method you use to get the guns out of the equation, if you are dealing with an individual who might harm you an abundance of caution is required.

Ok, you have all your preparation work done and you are on your way, the first 36 hours are very important in pulling this plan off with no mistakes.

When you leave do not have your car packed from floor to roof with stuff from your past, it looks suspicious and you might inadvertently take something that will link back to your old identity, make sure your car has no faulty lights, turn signals or anything else that would draw the attention of law enforcement.

If you have not done so, destroy all your old identification and cell phone.

Purchase a disposable cell phone for emergency use and change your appearance at this time. If you have a beard or moustache, shave it off, dye your hair or shave your head. Put on a pair of shades, a ball cap and hit the road.

Take secondary roads to avoid traffic surveillance cameras and highway patrol officers. Obey the posted speed limits and enjoy the scenic route.

CHAPTER 4

Big Brother is watching, close your curtains.

"No one likes to see a government folder with his name on it."

— *Stephen King*

Now that you are on your way, you need to be aware of all the ways we leave electronic and biological breadcrumbs for anyone to track your every move.

This chapter will attempt to give you an understanding of the most common types of surveillance techniques; and what you can do to counter them and protect your privacy.

The first and most used tracking device is the personal cell phone; it is always announcing to the cell phone network its location, even when it is off.

The method used to find you via your cell phone is called triangulation. It is used by law enforcement all the time, smart phones like the Apple, Android use GPS which is far more accurate than using cell phone towers.

Corporations have gotten into the mix also, if you have ever wondered why, you have gotten a text message or some other type of advertisement sent to your phone, it is because the advertisement company knows your location and they are trying to steer you to a business that is in your vicinity.

For instance, you get a text to get one dollar off a slice of pizza at Joe's Pizza Shop and Joe's Pizza Shop is across the street from your present location.

Cell phone companies sell your location for advertisement revenue and it is a very lucrative business, they will also give to any government agency under the flimsiest of pretense of almost anything they are presented with.

The only credible defense against this technology is to only use disposable cell phones and change them at regular intervals.

Most people who use the internet believe what they do online is anonymous; nothing could be further from the truth.

Each time your computer connects to the internet for any reason it is assigned an internet protocol address more commonly known as an ip address.

A computer ip address is as unique as a street address; in fact, your street address can be determined by your ip address.

Too many business and government websites try to collect personal information for no good reason other than it might be of value in the future.

The defense against this kind of data mining is to use a proxy service for web browsing or use the stealth or incognito settings on browsers like Firefox or Chrome.

To connect to the internet in the first place an internet service provider is needed, public WIFI hotspots are everywhere they usually are no cost to use, and no records are kept.

It is also possible to send email without it being tracked back to you by using an anonymous email server; you can find this free service on the internet with a quick Google search.

As was stated earlier; what you are doing is using disinformation to help cover your tracks and using techniques to undermine the technology used to monitor you.

Did you know the identification that you carry can be read while it is safely tucked away in your wallet or purse?

The scanner to do this is so inexpensive it is routinely used in taverns, night clubs etc.

An effective countermeasure to this type of snooping is to wrap your cards in aluminum foil, the same type you use in the kitchen.

This makes your cards undetectable also, an Altoid mint box will also work as well as foil. If your automobile has a built-in cell phone and GPS, you should consider figuring out how to disable it or get a vehicle that does not have those systems installed.

Law enforcement agencies do not have to plant a listening device in your home, car, or place of business any more all they must do is turn on the onboard cell phone and listen.

I have always thought that virtual assistants, smart speakers, smart tv's or any device in your home that listens or watches you is a bad idea, my wife thinks otherwise.

She believes I am a bit eccentric about these gadgets but after decades of marriage, I carefully pick my battles.

Another issue you need to be aware of is the biological identifiers that are unique to every human being that are deposited everywhere we go.

You will be sleeping in a motel along the way, do not sleep in the bed, bring along a sleeping bag and sleep on the floor.

You will not shed your skin in the bed leaving DNA evidence that you were at that location, this also goes for combing your hair, shaving etc.

The objective is to give the appearance that you in fact have vanished, you will be eating prepared food while you are in transit, do not go inside of a restaurant and have a sit-down meal, instead order take out.

The reason is, you would leave your DNA and fingerprints on the dining utensils and there is always the possibility someone might recognize you or the presence of video surveillance.

Surveillance cameras are inexpensive these days so consequently almost every type of business has them, to deal with them it was suggested you wear a pair of sunglasses and a hat, wig, or something to make it more difficult for facial recognition software to identify you.

Take note of how you walk and stand and change your posture and stride. There is software that analyzes your walk or gait and is very accurate in identification from just analysis of a person's stride, you might consider using a cane or crutch.

It is fine to wear sunglasses during the day even if you are inside, however sunglasses at night draw lots of attention of the kind you do not want.

Every item that is purchased from one of the big box stores or a major grocery store has a technology called RFID embedded in the packaging or in the item itself.

All foods should be removed from the store package and placed in plastic containers or bags, of course you throw the packaging away.

RFID does not require any power but can be read from quite a distance, this technology is making its way into just about any product you can imagine, remember "knowledge is power".

CHAPTER 5

A New Social Security Number.

"And all of it generates a data trail. All of it is trackable somewhere at some level, and much of it is traceable to this location."

— Kate O'Neill

The social security number was never intended to be a form of identification; however, it has morphed into the lynchpin of your identity.

Most everyone who you do any type of business with will ask for it. It is linked to your credit, employment, education, and other databases private and government.

Most people believe the social security number that is given to United States citizens at birth stays with them until death.

You can get a new one, there are times when requesting a new social security number make sense, for instance if you are the victim of identity theft and the thief has committed crimes and ran up huge debts using your social security number and you have exhausted all available avenues trying to repair your identity.

You could be fleeing from an individual or situation that is life threatening, perhaps you are a legal alien or immigrant, and your prospective employer or property owner requires a social security number.

These scenarios are routine and people who have the misfortune to find themselves in these situations can be issued a new social security number, yes, you will jump thru a few hoops, but you are dealing with the federal government and that is to be expected.

Assuming you have already changed your name, if your situation warranted that, you would need to provide documentation supporting this and a few other items of identification.

Take the time and effort, gather all your paperwork, and apply for a new number, under no circumstances make a number up or use another individual's number be they dead or alive.

You will need to obtain and complete Form SS-5, it is available on the Social Security Administration website or you can pick it up at your local Social Security office.

The process will go much smoother if you have everything, the agency is expecting. Some of the documents you can use to establish proof of citizenship are your current social security card, United States Passport, employee, school ID, or marriage certificate.

The objective of this is to establish your identity and proof of citizenship to the Social Security Administration.

If you are not a United States citizen the procedure is nearly identical, but the required documents are different.

They are a valid guest visa or passport; work permit or driver's license are the essential documents the Social Security Administration is looking for.

The more documentation you must have to demonstrate the validity of your request for a new social security number the better your chances of getting what you want.

If you have a history of being a victim of assault or domestic violence, get a police report, medical records, and photos if they are available of your bruises etc.

Letters from counselors, friends or coworkers corroborating your account of your situation is also helpful.

Being the victim of identity theft in some ways can be worse than a physical assault. Bruises will eventually heal but the consequences of a thief messing up your identity can drag on for years.

It is difficult to live with the kind of uncertainty identity theft hanging over your life brings your way.

People have spent time in jail because someone stole their identity and committed a crime.

Unfortunate victims of this type of crime have had to carry papers issued by various law enforcement agencies to prove who they are in the event of a routine traffic stop or some other routine interaction with law enforcement.

Yes, it could happen to you, a law-abiding citizen mistakenly jailed, even if you can straighten it out quickly, who wants to be bothered with that kind of trouble.

A new social security number is the ultimate and preferred solution to a bad case of identity theft.

The mechanics of getting a new social security number are straightforward a new number and social security card is given to you personally, meaning you must go to your local Social Security Administration office with all your documentation and a completed SS-5.

Once you get your new number do all you possibly can to safeguard it, again it is very important to the success of this undertaking to protect your new identity from linking back to your old identity.

The easiest way to ruin all that you have done is to use a credit card or account of any kind that belonged to your old identity. Starting over with a clean slate means exactly that.

If you co-mingle, your new identify with your old identity the credit bureaus will instantly flag your account and forever associate you with your old name and social security number.

To add insult to injury they will sell and share that information with whomever they choose because corporations do not have to respect your constitutional right to privacy.

The fourth amendment in the United States Constitution is supposed to protect the citizens from unwarranted searches and surveillance of their person and home.

The framers of the constitution had government abuse in mind when that amendment and several others that will not be discussed because they are not relevant to the subject matter being presented.

In their wildest dreams this nation's first politicians could not have imagined GPS, RFID, Cell Tower Triangulation and Video Cameras that see in total darkness and use facial recognition software. Their collective genius was "understanding" the need of a person to be left alone if that is their desire. It is a shame that they did not understand how powerful corporations that are not bound by the constitution would become.

CHAPTER 6
Build a credible past.

After you make your exit from your present life and identity, it will quickly become apparent that you must have some type of life story or narrative to explain who you are, where you grew up, attended high school, and did the stuff average people do.

All of us have a past and you will have to make one up; the more mundane and ordinary the better.

Strive to position yourself in the center of the bell-curve, so forget the stories about being a secret agent or in the witness protection program, or a stranded time traveler, you get the point.

The key to getting this part of your plan done right is "simplicity and consistency". The reason for simplicity is the less information you provide about your past the greater the chance of you being successful in keeping details you want private to remain that way.

The narrative you invent about yourself should consider your real-life situation, for instance if you are middle aged, it will not appear out of the ordinary to not have parents that are alive.

The older you are the longer your narrative must be, to span your life, longer but not more detailed.

The best way to construct your new past is to write it out, pretend you are writing a script for a movie or a New York Times bestselling novel.

After you have written your story, commit it to memory and do not change the story.

The more times you tell the same story the more natural it will sound, tell it for a long enough time you will begin to believe it yourself.

A common mistake made by individuals who otherwise had a well thought out and superbly executed new identity plan, was providing too much information about themselves.

Too much data voluntarily given up by you at best will make you look somewhat strange and in the worst-case scenario your past being discovered and the problems you escaped find you again.

You should not just sit down and dreamed up a new past, you will have to give this the same level of attention to detail that you gave to the other parts of your plan.

Your education history and employment history are the eight-hundred-pound gorilla in the room.

These two items are something you should prepare to deal with in a way that makes sense, because you will need to talk about employment history in a job interview and when you get the job your new coworkers are going to have a natural curiosity about you.

It is a bad idea to build your past where you will end up staying, pick a high school on the other side of the country or better still; pretend you were a military brat and attended school in foreign countries.

You must have an employment history unless you are a young person seeking entry-level employment.

It will not be difficult to create a credible resume today and appear to be one of our unfortunate citizens who became the victim of a plant closure, business bankruptcy or a displaced employee when the company outsourced your job to a foreign country.

Use your imagination to fill in the blanks but remember too detailed an explanation for almost anything that arouses suspicion in the person listening or observing you.

People are hard wired to share experiences and crave companionship; it is going to be tough for a while as you settle into your new life and identity.

You will have plenty of time for friends and fellowship after the dust has settled, and your day-to-day activities become as ordinary as any other citizens.

Until that day arrives, it is a bad idea for you to get to close or to let someone get to close to you emotionally while you are in this transitional period.

People often make bad choices when they let feelings short circuit their logical mind. At this stage of your plan, you do not want any unneeded distraction or trouble that might blind you to potential problems or cause you to not exercise due diligence because you feel lonely.

Grifters and con artists of various persuasions will steal your money and material assets.

As a rule, you can watch out for those types of persons and protect yourself from them, you also need to watch out for the individual who is toxic and an emotional and psychic vampire, not a movie monster vampire or a character from the series of romance novels aimed at teen girls.

You will know this type of person because of the way they make you feel. They will either pull you towards situations in a direction that is totally out of character for you, and they might convince you to do things that you would never consider but for the influence of this person.

This describes just one type of person to avoid; the other type of person to avoid gives off so much negative energy and pessimism that they change the mood and outlook of everybody they meet.

You will have to interact with people and that is a good thing, the world fortunately has more good people in it than bad or worse yet evil people.

This fact of life guarantees a better than fifty percent chance of all relationships working out in a positive way, the key is to start with a positive person.

Probably you will have to get a job doing something to support yourself in your new life, the ideal job for you is something that nobody in your past would imagine you doing to earn a living.

The fact that you are reading this book on a Kindle, PC, iPad, or some other tech platform proves you are comfortable with technology and it might be an area you could work in.

Use this unique twist of fate to go as far as your skill set will take you.

Remember, it is always helpful if you are doing something you enjoy supporting yourself.

If you repaired automobiles in your past life but you have always wanted to be a Chef, do it; there is no better time than now.

You have something many people only dream about, a clean slate and a fresh start.

CHAPTER 7

Find a place to live and get a job.

"I don't like to share my personal life… it wouldn't be personal if I shared it."

— George Clooney

Having a place to go to, not just a geographic area; an actual address, the home you will live in provides an enormous amount of psychological comfort and physical safety.

Shelter is a very important need; it is right behind the need for food and water; you must make provision for your shelter requirements yourself.

If you put your need for shelter in the hands of someone, you are going to be sexually exploited in exchange for a place to stay.

It does not matter if you are a male or female the same dynamic applies equally.

Young people are more of a target than older people for obvious reasons. This does not have to happen to you because earlier in the book you were instructed to sell as much stuff from your past life as possible, you want cash.

If your financial situation is like 99 percent of the population, money is something you rarely have enough of, when this is coupled with the temporary financial pressure of relocation; you have a recipe for stress and worry.

Again, success starts with a well thought out and executed plan before you make your move do some research and find out what the housing market is like at your destination.

The internet: should be one of the primary tools you use to find a home, you can find realtor listings, photographs, and a way to contact the owner to lease the property.

Once you find a couple of promising leads, use Google Earth to get a street view of the property.

This amazing free service will also allow you to take a virtual tour of the immediate neighborhood because you do not want to rent an oasis in the middle of a desert.

 Any additional information that will help you find a place you feel comfortable and safe in is a worthwhile investment of your time and effort.

Complete the rental agreement and handle the entire process online. Unfortunately, the internet is full of con artist, so it is important to make sure the person or entity you are dealing with is a reputable property manager or property management company.

It is better to spend a little more per month in rent to be near shopping, medical services, and possible places of employment.

Leave the backwoods to the people who choose to live off the grid because of mental or political reasons, those types are deeply suspicious of outsiders and probably would not welcome you anyway.

After you move in be a good neighbor and do not draw attention to yourself, dress and conduct yourself like the people around you.

Let people come to you to offer friendship or to satisfy their curiosity about you, remember telling people as little about yourself as possible is your goal.

If you let them talk, you will learn a lot about your new surroundings and the person doing the talking will appreciate you letting them brag about themselves.

You will also get some practical information like when garbage is picked up, if you can park your car on the street overnight, the best place to buy groceries and where to go to have a good time.

If you are a person of faith and practice one of the common religions, you could ask about local churches, temple, or mosque.

If you sense this is something your neighbor is a little reluctant to talk about, change the subject and move on.

It is better to give the impression that you are an upstanding moral person not a weekend partier.

There is an old saying "good fences make good neighbors" the fence does not necessarily have to be a real fence; it also can be interpreted to mean we must have boundaries in our life.

There is no good reason to become more than neighborly to quickly with anyone when you move into a new community as a matter of fact there is plenty of reason for the contrary.

Now that you have moved in, and you feel good about your selection of town and housing, it is time to get a job or figure out some other legal means to produce income.

If you have the inclination and expertise in some trade or vocation, give serious thought to starting your own business.

There are plenty of stories of people like Les Brown a world-famous motivational speaker and lecturer, who lived in his office while he built his business.

The internet is a platform that could launch an infinite number and type of businesses so let your imagination run free.

Not everybody is suited for entrepreneurship and that is ok, the economy would not and could not function without good employees.

You will have an easier time finding employment in a small business versus a large multinational corporation, the rate of pay is usually less at the small company and scrutiny of your past is generally less, so it all sort of balances out, less money and less hassle.

Another advantage in working for a small company is the opportunity for training and career development.

If you prove yourself to be an above average worker and demonstrate by your work performance that you care about the company the owner will do everything, they can, to keep you employed.

It does not matter which direction you choose; self-employment or a position as an employee in a company, it is going to be difficult for the first few months.

Even if you are an expert at what you are doing it is going to take some time for the temporary stress of something new and different in your life to abate.

Continue to be a wise steward of your money because it is a finite resource and most pay increases are not given until you have worked for three to six months, this also assumes your work and conduct have been satisfactory.

 At this point you have erased your identity and data from the internet, you have a new name, identity, social security number, a new home and job. Treat yourself to a bottle of your favorite beverage, you have done well.

CHAPTER 8

Opening Bank Accounts and Credit Card Accounts

"Nobody cares about you as a person, but they care about you as a customer. That's how business works."

— Abdallah Shawaf

It is almost impossible to manage your life without some type of Bank or Bank-like presence, this usually consist of a checking account, savings account, and credit card.

Fortunately, you have more options today than a similarly situated individual had in the not-too-distant past.

Several companies offer prepaid Visa, MasterCard and now American Express has jumped into the market with their version of prepaid card.

The prepaid credit card is easier to obtain than a checking account, however transaction fees vary so you must compare the products to determine what is the best deal.

Large retail operations like Wal-Mart market several financial products with low transaction fees.

This is not an endorsement of the company; Wal-Mart is mentioned only because their stores are in most cities and towns in this country.

The reason you should start with a new bank account and credit card is to prevent linking back to your past life and identity.

Starting fresh means exactly that, you cannot have any ties to your past life.

You will build a credit history over time with your new identity, pay your rent, utilities, and credit purchases on time every month and in as few as twenty-four to thirty-six months you will have a decent credit history.

Although a sizeable and growing amount of people prefer the new non-banks to traditional banks there is another option, credit unions; they tend to be more consumer friendly than traditional banks and cheaper to use than the new non-banks.

Credit Unions are cheaper to use because the members own them, you will have to investigate and find out what the membership requirements are for the credit union you want to join.

When you open your checking account the customer service representative will ask you; "what number do you want your checks start with," choose a number like 1005 or so.

Your objective is to make your checking account appear to have been active for a long period of time, if your chosen financial institution does not ask, tell them what you want and if they do not wish to comply with your request, think seriously about taking your business elsewhere.

You have way too many options in the personal banking realm, you do not have to tolerate an inflexible bank or credit union. It is your money and your choice. The internet is a major player in the consumer banking marketplace; there are several internet only banks.

Internet only means there are no brick-and-mortar branch offices to do banking transactions.

Your only option with a bank using this business model is their website or an ATM, for some people this is preferable because they work hours that make using a traditional bank or credit union difficult, they do not need the social interaction or anything else.

If you decide to use an online bank or the website of any financial institution there are some precautions, you should take.

Always use a strong password composed of special characters, numbers, blank spaces-, upper- and lower-case letters.

Change your password often, do not use a free Wi-Fi hotspot at a coffee shop or some other public place to do your banking or to transmit any sensitive data over an unsecured internet connection.

It is also a bad idea to do your banking on a computer that is connected to the internet all the time, this means a full-time cable or dsl connection.

This warning also applies to tablet computers, and smart phones. Most people do not understand that a smart phone is a computing device that happens to have an integrated phone, they are inherently insecure devices, you should not do banking on them.

All these devices should have antivirus software installed and updated as needed.

CHAPTER 9

Establishing New Friendships.

"A fish with his mouth closed never gets caught."

— Fuad Alakbarov

People are social animals, most of us need the company, companionship, and social validation group membership affords.

You are living a new life with a new identity; all your friends and associates must be new.

If you attempt to carry over any connection to your previous identity, you run the risk of your new life and identity you worked so hard build being compromised.

There are over 4 billion people on this planet; you will not have any problem finding new people to make friends and form new associations.

If you observe the dynamics of human relationships, you will notice that people have a tendency too group themselves into self-selected sects of likeminded folks.

This fact is why you need to make a conscious effort to avoid the types of people and activities you engaged in before you disappeared. Everybody has heard the expression "it's a small world", the world is not small, but it is viewed and experienced from the narrow vantage point of our likes and dislikes in people and leisure time activities.

The proliferation of social media websites creates a real possibility that someone who knew you in your past life might find you because you were pursuing or participating in activities inside of your comfort zone.

It would be a personal tragedy to find your photo on a Facebook page because you attended the local "bottle cap collectors" Christmas party.

Someone in your group could innocently post your photo and someone that you knew from your past recognizes you.

Avoid this; develop new interest, forge friendships and alliances with a different type of individual.

Now is the time to step out of your comfort zone, the obvious place to find friends is at work, since you will spend about one third of your day on the job this setting could be fertile territory.

You will be the new kid on the block and your coworkers will be watching you closely to figure you out and form an opinion about you as an individual and competent coworker.

If you are a person of faith finding a house of worship might be of some benefit to you in finding friends.

Churches, Mosque, Synagogues and Temples come in all sizes and have personalities as diverse as the populations they serve.

It might take some time to find a place you enjoy experiencing the inner peace and calm people of faith say they feel.

You have probably seen or heard commercials claiming that people have found their soul mate on "you fill in the blank" website.com.

This might work for you; however, you must never let your guard down, treat the individuals you meet in cyberspace with the same degree of caution you would exercise in the real world because the internet is full of conmen and Grifters of all sorts.

Stay cautious and avoid people, who are emotionally unstable, fortunately, they will be easy to spot because of some odd mannerism they will exhibit so pay close attention.

Your new neighbor might find you attractive, interesting or both and attempt to get to know you better, the point is people are everywhere and most are looking for someone, single or not.

Stay away from people who are married or encumbered in some other way, those situations always turn out badly.

You also need to examine your motives, if they are not well meaning do not take advantage of someone physically or emotionally, people are volatile when feelings and pride are involved.

This chapter has concentrated on advice to protect you from predators as you ease into a more normal routine, always remember it is wrong for you to harm another individual to satisfy yourself.

If someone is interested in you and you have no interest in them, please politely send them on their way while preserving their dignity.

They will appreciate it and you will feel good about doing the right thing. Love affairs gone wrong are frequently the genesis of stalking, property crimes, assaults, and manslaughter.

People are unpredictable and sometimes volatile, as was said earlier; proceed with caution.

CHAPTER 10

Stuff you will have to do forever.

"Very private people have mastered the art of telling you little about themselves but doing it in such a way you think you know a lot."

— Anonymous

It is great that you have successfully changed your life and identity, however there are some maintenance things that you will always need to watch out for.

The number one thing that will ruin all your work and plans is complacency.
It is easy to screw up when you become overconfident or sloppy.

In the beginning of this book, you were told, "the effort made to find you is directly proportional to the resources and the will of your pursuer to find you".

If the government is after you because you have broken the law, as was stated earlier the pursuit will not stop.

As federal agents retire, they will pass on your case file to their replacements, the US government has never stopped searching for DB Cooper and his case has been open for a few decades.

You can never contact family members; the reasons are the authorities or whomever is looking for you will be watching your family and past close associates.

The other reason is you vanished from the lives of people you had relationships with on some level.

It does not matter if they were private or professional, the fact is you disappeared, and they had to do whatever was required to move on.

They have filled in the hole in their life you left when you vanished; you will not be welcomed back.

You must not stalk or engage in any type of surveillance activity on people from your past life this is a blanket statement, do not friend them thru social media, post cryptic messages on blogs they might have, email, or attempt to get in relative proximity of them.

They will sense it; we all have had that feeling that someone is staring or following us. A strong emotional connection seems to be the catalyst, it could be love or hate they are both intense emotions.

There is no scientific explanation for that special awareness we all seem to have, maybe it is a left-over evolutionary adaptation designed to protect our species from predators. The point is you will be discovered, and your plans ruined, do not chance it.

Stay away from your past, all of it. If you were the target of violence prone individuals or a criminal gang, the necessity of keeping a low profile is obvious.

Keeping a low profile does not mean spending the rest of your life in the shadows; it means being aware of your surroundings and the implications of your actions and how that relates to your present status.

Some people have no problem leading a quiet life never drawing attention to themselves, on the other hand if you are the type of person who must be the center of attraction in whatever venue you happen to be in, you are going to have trouble.

Pursue high visibility endeavors at your peril, local political office, church official, sports team coach or star player might bring you the ego soothing attention you crave but the downside is increased scrutiny from the people who will sing your praises and the folks who are envious and want to see you fail or fall.

Keep your photo out of newspapers and off the internet, do no evil and do good anonymously. There are people among us that need the public admiration of others like plants need water and sunshine.

If you are one of those individuals and know you will not thrive without the adulation of throngs of fans, a successful disappearance might not be possible in this country.

 A successful plan for you might be centered in your choosing another country to start over in.

The principles and techniques explained in this book can be applied anywhere on this planet, the most important point to take away from this chapter is to stay as inconspicuous as possible.

If you do decide to remake your life in a foreign country, you will probably have an easier time acquiring identity papers and other supporting documents.

If you make the effort to assimilate into the culture and norms of your new surroundings, the odds of you living out a quiet and peaceful life are very good.

The choice is yours, to successfully not be found by employing the strategies and techniques laid out in this book or hope to be lucky.

CHAPTER 11

Leave The country, disappear abroad.

"Americans don't care about privacy, and the people running the country couldn't be happier." — Thor Benson

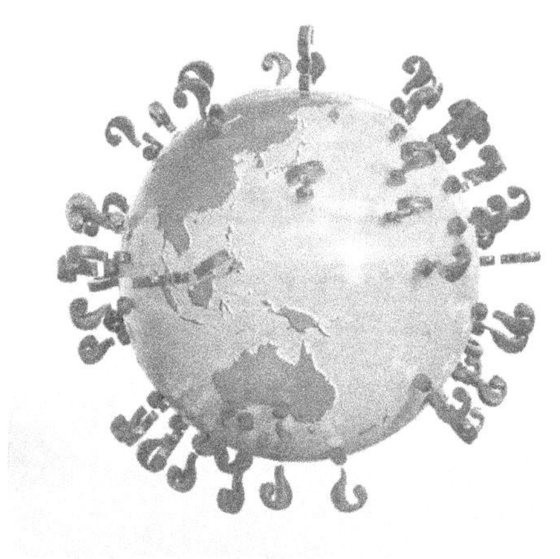

This is the most extreme option available to you but could be the most effective way to disappear especially if law enforcement is after you and you have the resources to escape.

This is not an endorsement of the idea of becoming an international fugitive but if you are being pursued for something you are innocent of or being persecuted for political reasons you might have to run.

Edward Snowden would be in a federal prison today if he had not fled to Russia, Bill Cosby would be free today if he had fled to France.

The film director Roman Polanski was accused of similar crimes and is living free in France today. He can not set foot on American soil but in my opinion, that might be better than prison.

The source of your problem could be something like a new law that makes your business a criminal enterprise, you are a controversial activist, or have made enemies of some very bad people like drug lords.

Circumstances like that would make most people want to disappear.

If you had to get out of the country, there are places you could go and places you should stay away from.

You need to make sure your destination is a place where you are not at risk of being extradited back to the United States as the U.S. has bilateral extradition agreements with over 107 countries.

Extradition: When one country sends an individual, who is accused or convicted of a crime back to the country where it was committed or alleged to have been committed.

It involves a bilateral treaty based upon the cooperation of law enforcement agencies of both countries.

Extradition Treaties: An extradition treaty is an official agreement between two nations using a mutual agreement to extradite fugitives back to their respective country to face legal consequences.

There are many instances where countries that have extradition treaties, do not followed them, and times when countries that do not, have extradition treaties have sent fugitives back anyway.

The extradition process has a lot of political smoke that swirls around it. There are on average 400-700 people that are extradited back to the United States every year.

You stand a much better chance at longtime freedom if you choose to hide out in a country that does NOT have an official extradition treaty with the United States.

Countries with No Extradition Treaty with the U.S

Afghanistan, Algeria, Andorra, Angola, Armenia, Azerbaijan, Bahrain, Bangladesh, Belarus, Benin, Botswana, Brunei, Burkina Faso, Burundi, Cambodia, Cameroon, Cape Verde, Central African Republic, Chad, China, Comoros, Congo, Djibouti, East Timor, Equatorial Guinea, Eritrea, Ethiopia, Gabon, Georgia, Guinea, Guinea-Bissau, Indonesia, Ivory Coast, Kazakhstan, Kuwait, Kyrgyzstan, Laos, Lebanon, Libya, Madagascar, Maldives, Mali, Mauritania, Moldova, Mongolia, Morocco, Mozambique, Namibia, Nepal, Niger, Oman, Qatar, Russia, Rwanda Samoa, São Tomé & Príncipe, Saudi Arabia, Senegal, Solomon Islands, Somalia South Sudan, Sudan, Taiwan,

Tajikistan, Togo, Tunisia, Turkmenistan, Uganda, Ukraine, UAE, Uzbekistan, Vanuatu, Vatican City, Vietnam, Yemen

The Best Non-Extradition Countries

If you are interested in a country that has first world infrastructure, medical, housing etc. these countries should fit the bill.

This list of countries is not all inclusive, they were chosen based on economic growth, political stability and modern infrastructure.

Russia and China are at the top of the list of non-extradition countries. Neither of them has extradition treaties with the US.

In addition to that, both have a history of tension with the US, so are unlikely to want to hand you over.

One famous case of non-extradition in Russia is that of Edward Snowden who was able to find asylum there.

Both Russia and China can be ideal places to reside for both short-term and long-term.

They are affordable, and their vast size and diversity mean that you can live any kind of lifestyle that suits your preferences and budget.

Brunei is one of the richest countries on the list of nations with no extradition treaty. The Sultan of Brunei does not take orders from anyone and does not take kindly to outside interference.

Ethiopia, Botswana, and Tunisia are three good countries which do not have extradition treaties. Ethiopia and Botswana are two of the strongest economies on the African continent.

The North African nation of Tunisia is home to a rapid growing economy and middle class it also has excellent weather.

Vietnam, Cambodia, And Laos are rapidly growing countries without extradition treaties. Vietnam and Cambodia are especially popular tourist and business destinations.

Here, you can enjoy a high quality and affordable lifestyle, the people will make you feel very welcome. These countries have better internet speed than the US with many business opportunities available.

Ukraine And Moldova These two fast-growing Eastern European offer good investment opportunities in their up-and-coming economies.

Ukraine is also a good jurisdiction for offshore banking. Most importantly, neither of them has extradition treaties with the US.

Montenegro the small Balkan country of Montenegro is a beautiful and unique country it offers a great lifestyle and good investment opportunities.

Unlike its neighbors, Serbia and Croatia, Montenegro does not have an extradition treaty with the US. It is also not a part of the EU which means it offers a certain degree of financial privacy.

Become a citizen of the country you are hiding in!

Having dual citizenship allows you to become a citizen of two or more countries at the same time.

While not all countries allow you to hold two (or more) passports at the same time such as India or China, most countries such as the USA, Canada and the UK allow it.

There are also those countries where it's a grey zone, like Germany, Panama, and Singapore where it is generally not allowed in theory though often done in practice.

1. Ancestry

Many countries allow you to easily acquire citizenship if you can prove that you have ancestral ties. This is especially prevalent in parts of Europe.

For some countries, you need to prove that your parents were born there, but for others you can qualify for ancestral citizenship if your grandparents or great grandparents were born there.

Citizenship by ancestry is usually free or at low cost, the process can be finished relatively quickly and is undoubtedly the best way to obtain citizenship if you qualify.

Law of Return Citizenship

Israel offers one of the fastest and easiest paths to obtaining dual citizenship under their "Law of Return".

 This option is available for all Jewish individuals or those with Jewish ancestry. This even includes those who convert to Judaism.

Those seeking Israeli citizenship under the Law of Return are eligible within a few months after entering Israel.

It is important to consider whether Israeli citizenship is indeed right for you, Israeli citizens are forbidden from entering certain Islamic countries, and there is a long history of complex politics and foreign relations.

Furthermore, Israeli citizens are officially required to serve in the military for a certain period, however this may be waived in some situations. It is important to confirm whether this would be a requirement.

2. **Naturalization**

The process of acquiring citizenship by naturalization usually involves living in a country for a specific number of years as a permanent resident before qualifying to apply for full citizenship.

 Obtaining permanent residency is the first step which usually requires spending more than 183 days a year for x number of years.

Requirements for obtaining full citizenship can vary greatly from country to country.

You could qualify for citizenship in as little as three years in some cases (e.g., Paraguay, Armenia, Dominican Republic), or well over 10 years in other cases (Germany, Austria, Switzerland).

The specific requirements regarding how much time you need to spend in the country, whether you need to establish economic ties, know the language, history or constitution depends upon the country.

Remember, finding a foreign country to become a citizen of is totally different than trying to stay out of reach of a government trying to snatch you back to answer for something you have done or are being accused of.

Panama is the easiest place in the world to establish residency under the Panama 'Friendly Nations Visa'.

It is a straightforward process that involves setting up a local company and opening a bank account with a small sum.

You do not even have to spend time in the country and after five years, you are eligible to apply for naturalization.

Naturalization is the most time-consuming way to become a dual citizen, thankfully it not your only option.

However, this option makes the most sense if you can afford to put down roots and wait the required time.

3. Marriage

Citizenship by marriage is another route to naturalization, in my opinion this is the worst way to attempt to gain citizenship. Most countries in the world will give you a second passport if you marry a citizen of your host country. This is the case in Canada, Ireland, France, and the United States.

The temptation to marry somebody to obtain citizen must be resisted, participating in a sham marriage arrangement is a problem you do not need.

Not only can you get in trouble and kicked out by the government if you are caught but you are easy prey to extortion by the arranged spouse.

4. Investment

A multitude of countries will let you buy yourself citizenship or minimally put you at the front of the line by offering what is known as citizenship by investment or economic citizenship.

This process is aimed at individuals who are looking to acquire dual citizenship in the fastest and easiest way possible.

In exchange for a real estate purchase or an economic donation anywhere around $100,000 USD Dominica and Vanuatu grant upwards of 1-2 million requests for citizenship. The countries of Malta and Cyprus will grant you a passport in as little as   3-6 months.

In fact, you can cut your citizenship processing time in Vanuatu, for an extra $10,000 USD and get it in 30 days making it the fastest citizenship by investment in the world.

It sounds corrupt but money has always bought access to people that have it. There are generally no residency requirements or any minimum number of days that you are required to live there per year.

Just pay your money and all is well, in fact, you do not even need to visit the country beforehand, it can all be done online, the citizenship lasts for life and can be passed down to your descendants.

The most popular places to 'buy' second citizenship or golden visas are the Caribbean Island nations. For the price of a luxury car, there are about five options available in the Caribbean and they are generally the simplest and most affordable to obtain.

If you choose to pursue citizenship in the Caribbean, you also reap a big financial benefit as most islands in that part of the world have no taxes.

All the passports are high quality allowing 140+ countries you can visit with visa-free travel, together with the ability to live in some of the most picturesque and loveable destinations in the world.

If you are looking to gain citizenship by investment, you should consider these island nations: the locations are beautiful, and the price is right.

St. Kitts & Nevis

Dominica

Vanuatu

Malta

They all have official economic citizenship programs or golden passport opportunities that can be purchased through a real estate investment or a donation of upwards of 100,000-150,000 USD depending on the country.

If you are flexible with your time and lifestyle you can obtain citizenship in one of these places at relatively little cost.

Benefits of Dual Citizenship

Some of the benefits of getting a second passport are:

Better quality of life: Some countries are simply better to live in than others, I know it is heresy to say that but that does not make it untrue.

Most developed countries have better education, health care, mass transit, a meaningful social safety net and almost no gun problem.

Many of the countries that offer convenient ways to obtain dual citizenship happen to be in beautiful locations and are affordable.

Increased Freedom of Movement

In uncertain times, having a second passport can be a perfect backup plan in case you face uncomfortable living circumstances at home.

The dangerous and damaging consequences of political or economic upheavals, martial law, capital controls, and unchecked violence can all be mitigated knowing that you have a solid exit plan, the option of a second passport is often the perfect solution.

Tax Optimization

Many countries that offer dual citizenship also include 0% taxation possibilities.

It is possible to greatly minimize or even completely eradicate your tax burden by obtaining dual citizenship in a tax haven.

Countries such as Antigua or Vanuatu for instance, make it possible to live in the country without having to pay income or capital gain tax.

Each country has its own rules about taxation, and it may not be possible to completely avoid taxation, it will likely depend upon the second passport that you hold.

Investment Opportunities

Having dual citizenship opens a new world of potentially profitable of business and investment opportunities in your new country of citizenship, as well as other places in the world.

Live Long and Prosper

Now that you have read this book, you know how to plan your own disappearance and have a pretty good chance of becoming a ghost.

You learned to use misdirection, how to not leave biological or digital data breadcrumbs.

You learned the proper way to enter and blend into a new community, how to establish a new identity with proper documentation, find housing and employment.

You learned the reason to create a new past and stick to it and why you must never have anything to do with your past life.

If moving abroad is something you had in mind, the best places on Earth are listed and why you should consider them.

99% of the people who read this book will never have to act on the information shared, that is a good thing. Information is important to have because you never know, I hope you had as good a time reading this book as I had writing it.

Please take the time to review this book, click this link.

Best Wishes,
VL Ricketts

The End

Acknowledgements

Many thanks to my wife and soul mate
Diana for her boundless devotion,
understanding, nurturing, and keeping
me around for decades.

Books by VL Ricketts

Coming Soon!